The Donald Trump Way
The best business strategies from the king

1. Introduction
2. You are a brand and the main communicator of it.
3. Never depend on only one income source.
4. Know and believe in your brand.
5. Create your principles and stick to them.
6. Take calculated risks.
7. Surround yourself with excellence.
8. Be open to new ideas.
9. Time and energy are your main assets for success.
10. Know the system inside out and take advantage of it
11. Be in the right time at the right moment
12. You will fail, you better learn from it.
13. Have passion and love for what you do.
14. Between being consistent and being loud, choose being loud
15. Don't waver, keep your goal in mind and go for it!

1
Introduction

"If you are going to achieve anything, you have to take action. But action is just a small part of it."

Donald Trump

Congratulations on getting "The Trump Way", a book in which you will find out the secrets that have made Donald Trump one of the richest men in the world. He may be one of the most polarizing characters in the public eye, but his talent for business is undeniable, as he has proved by building the biggest real estate empire in the world.

But don't let the limelight fool you, Mr. Donald Trump is on it for the exposure and marketing. A good entrepreneur always knows how to get the most out of any situation he is involved in and Mr. Trump is the best at it. Most of the times it's because he has chosen to place himself there, but in other cases, a series of events led him to be under the spotlight and he has just figured out how to take advantage of the situations.

In any case he comes out triumphant and now you will know how to make it too. No matter what your situation is right now, you will be able to create and grow your own business or personal brand thanks to the lessons that Donald Trump has showed over the years.

As Trump says, action is a part of the equation, but just a small part. In this book you will find out which are the remaining parts and understand how everything works behind the curtains.

Get ready to make a paradigm shift and go through the following pages with an open mind, because you are on your way to make business like our millionaire mentor.

2
You are a brand and the main communicator.

Donald Trump is a one-man media company. If you pay attention to many of his interviews you will see he has amazing communication skills and this is the main reason why he gets so much attention.

Now, you should understand that you are a brand by yourself. You are the image of your business and your own personality will convey what it represents. You will evolve during time and your business skills as well, you'll learn new things, start new companies or brands. And when you do, why would you leave all the amazing work you put in behind? Thus, instead of starting over and over again when you participate in a new venture, you will integrate it to your always-growing personal brand; you can keep it all, if you stick to your essence.

Trump has mostly done it with his name (Trump Towers, Trump University, Trump Hotels, Trump Golf Courses) but, as proved in his successful campaign for the Republican Presidential Nomination, you can do it with your image as well, as long as you create a unique personality and brand for yourself.

In the age of social media, you are the main communicator of your brand. You will create the content for it and advertise it with your own actions. Whether is on TV interviews, Facebook, Twitter, Snapchat or Instagram, you are the leader of communications for all your brands and the front name on them is your name.

"Business rule number one: if you don't tell people about your success they probably won't know about it.

A few months ago I picked up 'The Art of the Deal', skimmed a bit and then read the first and last paragraphs I realized that after 17 years, they still rang true. I could have written these words yesterday."

Donald Trump

Once you've made a deal, the only way it's going to be worth anything is to then attract customers, he says. Similarly, creating a public persona helps you get the most out of your next deals.

Trump says that he's always embraced a healthy dose of sensationalism and controversy to pique the media's interest.

"I play to people's fantasies," he writes. "People may not always think big themselves, but they can still get very excited by those who do. That's why a little hyperbole never hurts. People want to believe that something is the biggest and the greatest and the most spectacular."

A lover of self-promotion, Mr. Trump admits that truth should never get in the way of closing a deal. He certainly has proven himself to be a master dealmaker and genius negotiator, but time and time again, he has stretched the truth to attract investors.

"Over the years I've participated in many battles and have really almost come out very, very victorious every single time," said Trump at the 2011 Conservative Political Action Conference. Apparently, Trump doesn't count his multiple business failings and bankruptcies as blemishes on his record.

So you must start this very moment, today, right now: Every day, every minute you wait, is lost money, lost time, lost chance. Stop waiting, preparing and getting ready and just get out there and do it already. Every time you procrastinate is time and effort wasted.

It doesn't matter how talented you are or how much you practice your craft and hone your skills. If you aren't out there doing the stuff you're good at (or getting good at), none of it matters.

Are you ready? Go!

Let's now see the steps you need to take to brand yourself and/or your business:

Step 1: Prelaunch

Start talking about what you are going to do. This is a Prelaunch and everyone loves the excitement around Trump revealing a new casino or golf course. Fans, media, colleagues, they all show up to "the event" as the amazing "plan" is unveiled. It gets almost as much media attention as the actual reveal on opening day.

This in fact not only is great for promoting your brand, but it also helps finding your audience or adjusting to your target market before even starting to put any work on it.

Step 2: Promote while doing it

Trump doesn't wait for something to be "finished" to start promoting it. Marketing continues while the project is "under construction."

Yes, hard work at your office and putting the effort to create something is a very time-consuming activity, but you have to prepare yourself and make some space in you schedule to network, to attend events and share your vision.

It's like movies do with their trailers and teasers. They build anticipation while working on the movie. And you should do the same with your projects.

Step 3: Use controversy in your favor

Controversy can, in a positive way, boost buzz and force people to talk about your brand. Controversy opens up discussion. It makes people think, and it provides notoriety for topics that may otherwise be unnoticeable. Use controversy to your advantage by engaging in friendly debates, defend your position on a particular topic, or better yet, get into the conversation with your brand as the solution of a certain problem. Remember, controversy is good if you can provide value within it.

Step 4: Be social, be where your audience is

Social channels are utmost important when trying to connect with all kinds of demographics. Trump understands the importance of giving everyone the means to follow his campaign and to connect with him, in the way that suits them best. Yes, there are the news and the TV are still the main source of information for the mainstream public, but more and more people are looking now at their smartphone screen than any other screen in the room.

Understand how each social channel works and use it to communicate your brand message. Remember, Facebook, Twitter and Snapchat are now the biggest social media platforms available and they all attend to different demographics.

3

Never depend on one income source.

When Donald Trump announced his candidacy for president, he made it clear that the majority of his fortune was made in real estate. But the truth is that he has many different income sources.

When Trump started as a New York developer, he made deals around luxury hotels, and that was a clear and renowned success. Then he branched out to golf courses, retail products, education, a tv show and pretty much anything you can imagine, even an energy drink in Israel. To mirror his diversification strategy, think of every new arena as just one part of a massive expansion, a new stepping stone for the big brand that.

Trump has been so successful mostly because he has managed to build a lifestyle brand around his luxurious and successful lifestyle, one that most people aspire to.

Work hard to cultivate this kind of image around your brand, use it to expand into new business opportunities and find new ways that you can profit from that. Just like Trump made with his books, his golf courses, or even his casinos. Choose your next ventures very carefully so that they match your brand's core values or that you can adapt to them.

When managing your brand or business, you must understand that core comprehension is very important before acquiring a new income source. You need to understand what is your brand most recognized for and use that in your favor to extend this knowledge to your new acquisitions.

The main reason to diversify your income is that you will always have safety. If one of your incomes suddenly falls apart, you will still have one or more extra to support you.

The lesson here is clear: Trump, a smart guy, has built his portfolio around real estate, because that's what he knows best but using that knowledge as a platform he's managed to expand his array of ventures to other areas, although never too far away to the things he knows best until he masters and new arena. You should do the same. Of course, at first you'll have to invest on a much smaller scale but little by little you will be able to expand your interests and your business ventures and maybe one day match Mr. Trump's themselves.

CNBC reported Trump earned about $9.5 million in royalty for his branded vodka, hotels, bottled water and energy drinks in the last 18 months. Trump also earned income for speaking fees, including $450,000 for three speeches he gave for ACN Inc.

The Wall Street Journal reported that he earned $8.6 million for operating an ice rink in New York City's Central Park and $580,000 from running a New York City carousel. His 15 golf courses earned him $176.4 million. He even earns an annual pension of $110,000 from the Screen Actors Guild, thanks to his TV appearances.

This is a good lesson. Sure, the skating rink in the biggest city in the United States is not going to be your next business. But Mr. Donald Trump is showing how important it is to have several income streams at one time.

Very few people have emergency funds or savings in case something goes wrong. Finding different ways to bring extra cash is always a great defense against unexpected unemployment, emergencies or even if you want to take a break from your job.

The majority of your income will probably come from one full-time job. But having a full-time job is no excuse not to invest in the stock market, savings bonds or other investment vehicles. This is an easy way to improve your income.

Some people also turn to smaller side jobs as an extra way to bring income into their budget.

And remember:

"Never get too attached to one deal or one approach... Keep a lot of balls in the air, because most deals fall out, no matter how promising they seem at first."
Donald Trump

4

Know and believe in your brand.

A study of voters' perceptions conducted by the Kellogg School and Brand Imperatives indicates that Trump supporters find him to be "Straightforward," "Smart," "Strong" and "Bold." He is effectively leveraging the brand crafted before this presidential race, during his days on "The Apprentice." He is about "telling it like it is" and "winning" by being "huge." His consistent penchant for action and love for exaggeration are part of what makes him memorable.

This perception was created in the audience because Donald Trump is consistent. He can be called crazy, criticized or even insulted and he remains exactly the same. From the sweeping, provocative statements to his willingness to alienate entire populations to his instantly recognizable speaking style, we get what we expect.

That is because he knows and believes in his brand. Is exactly the same as when you go to McDonald's and you know what kind of food to expect no matter where in the world you are in.

The more you believe in your brand, the more consistent you will be, even in the toughest situations. Strong brands deliver on what they promise.

Now, when Trump says he will make America great again – whether by building a wall, or changing taxes or any seemingly crazy plan he explains– he says it with such conviction that it seems plausible.

His followers don't doubt that he'll deliver. Confidence is one of the most attractive brand attributes there is. People follow and buy from brands or business that they trust.

To build your brand – and your following – you have to be consistent and confident about it.

"The final key to the way I promote is bravado. I play to people's fantasies. People may not always think big themselves, but they can still get very excited by those who do. That's why a little hyperbole never hurts."

Donald Trump

Therefore, you have to always think big of yourself. That way, you can get those around you excited by your brand or business. Make sure to always play to the people's fantasies.

You will get criticized along the way. That's an issue you won't be able avoid. Accept it and take it easy.

"Criticism is easier to take when you realize that the only people who aren't criticized are those who don't take risks."

Enjoy every piece of information that help you know better and believe more in your brand. Remember that the journey is one of the most important things in the business world. Or as Donald Trump would say:

"Think how boring it would be to just sail into things and have everything be perfect. You can't prove your merit on quiet waters, whether you're a businessman or a mariner."

5

Create your own principles and stick to them.

"When someone crosses you, my advice is 'Get Even!' That is not typical advice, but it is real life advice. If you do not get even, you are just a schmuck! When people wrong you, go after those people because it is a good feeling and because other people will see you doing it. I love getting even. I get screwed all the time. I go after people, and you know what? People do not play around with me as much as they do with others. They know that, if they do, they are in for a big fight."

Donald Trump

Having principles doesn't mean to be all nice and naive with everyone. What it means is that you have an established position for you, for your brand and for your business.

So, it's very important that you take your time to think and generate the principles that you will follow in your business ventures, since they are the ones crafting the path that you will have to take in order to create a very clear brand identity.

"I think the big problem this country has is being politically correct. I've been challenged by so many people, and I frankly don't have time for total political correctness. And to be honest with you, this country doesn't have time either."

Donald Trump

And just like Trump, you have to be honest with yourself and with your market or audience. People's bullshit-meter nowadays is very fine-tuned and they can see through anything that is not authentic. Remember, it can be very positive or negative but it has to be real.

"If Hillary Clinton can't satisfy her husband, what makes her think she can satisfy America?" **(deleted Twitter post, 2015)** There couldn't be a better example than this one.

But being faithful to your own principles doesn't mean that is all you can believe in, as you can see, Donald Trump is also a very religious man, but has chosen a church that suits his views. He sticks to what he believes in and you should too.

"People are so shocked when they find ... out I am Protestant. I am Presbyterian. And I go to church and I love God and I love my church."

And he always remains firm in his beliefs.

"I think the institution of marriage should be between a man and a woman. I do favor a very strong domestic-partnership law that guarantees gay people the same legal protection and rights as married people. I think it's important for gay couples who are committed to each other to not be hassled when it comes to inheritance, insurance benefits and other simple everyday rights."

Remember, any time you are challenged on your principles, the only way to get out of the situation with the victory on your hands is to stick to them. They will mark the way to go in confusing or hard times.

"You should never lose your cool unless it's an act...Never lose your cool unless you have a reason for doing so."

We can see in this example from his personal Twitter account:

*"Amazing how the haters & losers keep tweeting the name 'F**kface Von Clownstick' like they are so original & like no one else is doing it."*

At first, you would believe he is gone mad, perhaps angry, but Trump always keeps his cool. And he enjoys annoying his enemies while making them show their weak spots.

"My twitter has become so powerful that I can actually make my enemies tell the truth."

Trump haters are constantly scared because they lose. That is what you have to aim for.

6

Take calculated risks.

"Sometimes by losing a battle you find a new way to win the war."

Donald Trump

Your brand or business will take a hit or two along the way, but you have to pay close attention onto which are going to help you on the long run.

The thing is, if you don't take any risks, you will most likely end up failing, because it means your business is not moving fast enough to keep the pace of current times.

This is why Donald Trump makes a very important emphasis on this matter. Because you have to be always analyzing, studying, researching, knowing what ways are going to benefit the business or brand even if they seem risky at the beginning.

"You have to think anyway, so why not think big?"

This statement of Donald Trump sounds louder than ever. As the head of your business, you will always be facing difficult choices, but the whole idea behind taking calculated risks is that you are always thinking big about the long run, not the immediate effect.

"I have made the tough decisions, always with an eye toward the bottom line. In the end, you're measured not by how much you undertake but by what you finally accomplish."

But make no mistake, this doesn't mean that you have to be risking everything again and again, or that you should be pushing when you are in a closed alley. No. It is not always about doing it, sometimes is about not doing it what represents the calculated risk, or as Donald Trump Would say:

"Part of being a winner is knowing when enough is enough. Sometimes you have to give up the fight and walk away, and move on to something that's more productive."

Or:

"Experience taught me a few things. One is to listen to your gut, no matter how good something sounds on paper. The second is that you're generally better off sticking with what you know. And the third is that sometimes your best investments are the ones you don't make."

As we saw in the chapter before, stick to your principles and your instincts. Maybe you don't have all the experience required to make a new venture, then you have to be blatantly honest with yourself and think if this is something you can do or if it's better to pass on the opportunity because it has way more risks than benefits for your business.

Sometimes you will be in a situation where you are not the only one to decide or maybe the people around you will try to influence your business decision, whenever that happens remember always to put your business or brand first. Just like Donald Trump does.

"Everybody has their detractors. Some people say arrogance, or whatever they may say. I only have one thing in mind, and that's doing a great job for the country."

"Everything I do in life is framed through the view of a businessman. That's my instinct. If I go into a pharmacy to buy shaving cream, then I'm going to look for the best deal on shaving cream."

And learn from one of the common mistakes Donald Trump has made in the past:

"I'm competitive, and I love to create challenges for myself. Maybe that's not always a good thing. It can make life complicated."

7

Surround yourself with excellence.

Building an empire is not an easy task. Sure, you may have to begin alone and work hard on your own on the very first months of this amazing journey. But as time passes and, if you follow the strategies of this book and Mr. Trump himself, soon you will find yourself with a growth that you won't be able to handle with just two hands.

Therefore, you should understand what it means from the beginning: you will have to delegate. Even better, with modern technology you can outsource pretty much anything, from the logo of your company to a full-working customer service, lawyers, accountants, etc.

As Donald Trump states:

"You can't know it all. No matter how smart you are, no matter how comprehensive your education, no matter how wide ranging your experience, there is simply no way to acquire all the wisdom you need to make your business thrive."

Access to professionals in any area you need is easy nowadays, the hard part is to identify the good ones. There lies the key to your success after you let some parts of your business out of your hands. You will need people in which you can trust and who are well prepared for the job.

As Donald Trump said:

"What separates the winners from the losers is how a person reacts to each new twist of fate."

You have to be able to recognize those who are capable of producing under pressure because, let's face it, when you are a big player you will constantly be under the spotlight.

All professional interaction leads to knowledge. And if you surround yourself with excellence, there is a great chance you learn new things you had no idea were useful for your personal arsenal.

Just like Donald Trump mentioned in the media: *"Watch, listen, and learn. You can't know it all yourself. Anyone who thinks they do is destined for mediocrity."*

And you have something to give too. Don't be greedy in your knowledge; at the end of the day, the people you instruct are the one who are going to help your brand or business grow.

What's the point of having great knowledge and keeping them all to yourself?

And sometimes surrounding yourself with excellence is not only about education and knowledge, since you can teach the ones around you, it's also a matter of loyalty. Just like it happens in all of Donald Trump's business, according to the man himself - *"Partnerships must have loyalty and integrity at their core."*

As always, when in doubt, follow Donald Trump's motto:

"I only work with the best."

8

Be open to new ideas.

We all like to think that our opinion and ideas are always the best. It is even healthy to do so, but in business we always have to be smarter and sometimes being so means be open to new concepts that you can benefit from.

The fast pace of marketing trends and the new distribution channels are always challenging. Let's take the example of print media.

Let's imagine you have always dreamed about having your own magazine. Donald Trump also did in some point of his career.

Now imagine you join forces with a young and talented partner that suggests you should make your magazine, but because in today's world, print media is on its way to the cemetery, he believes the best way to do it is on the internet, digitally, so everyone can read in their tablets and phones.

Well the stubborn move would be to stick to your guns, make the print magazine and most likely fail.

The smart move however is to be open to this new idea, research about the possibilities it might give you and make an informed decision whether to make it print or digital. In this case I would save you the research: the better choice of course is go digital since all eyeballs are there now. And more eyeballs means more business.

Of course, going through this path is not going to be easy, especially if you are not a computer programmer, but as Donald Trump says:

"Courage is not the absence of fear. Courage is the ability to act effectively, in spite of fear."

And when you are in business you have to have the courage and intelligence to be open to new ideas.

Plus, it will be also helpful to promote your brand or business. Why, you may ask? Well…

"If you are a little different, or a little outrageous, or if you do things that are bold or controversial, the press is going to write about you."

Now let's make something clear. There will be times in which new ideas or even your own will fail. You may be criticized, but always, always remember Donald Trump's words:

"Criticism is easier to take when you realize that the only people who aren't criticized are those who don't take risks."

"You have to leave your comfort zone." Donald Trump did not make billions of dollars by just sticking to the one thing he loves the most, Real Estate, but he has tried as many things as possible.

Of course, some of them have failed, you can't have a 1.000 batting average, but the important thing here is that he's always pushing the boundaries of his comfort zone and, as we saw in the last chapter, if you are surrounded by excellence, success is an obvious result. But you have to keep pushing or your business will fail.

9

Time and energy are your main assets for success.

Your whole life is about time and energy, therefore your business is too. These are the main two assets you should always have no matter what your education level or your job are. You will always have a determined amount of time and energy.

So, you have to be wise on how to spend these two in order to receive the maximum amount of ROI (Return Of Investment) possible.

And the best way to do it is to always focus on solutions. Let's say you have a big debt, just like Donald Trump had in the past. The easy way and what most people do is focusing their time and energy on the problem, on the debt itself.

This is why most people fail when doing business. What you have to do instead is placing that exact time and energy in how to solve the problem instead.

Just like Donald Trump says:

"The image of success is important, but even more important is the ability to focus on solutions instead of on problems. That way, you'll never be thinking like a loser, and you probably won't look like one either."

Everything changes with this approach, even the image you have of yourself.

When Donald Trump was asked what he would do if he had to do it all over again, his one-line reply was: *"I would get into network marketing."*

Why? Simple you should focus your time and energy networking. This will give you more knowledge of your industry, more connections and more opportunities to find better deals or partnerships.

Even if you are starting, you can find an investor if you are networking. Remember chapter 1: **You are a brand and the main communicator of it**.

So communicate. Yes at the beginning it may seem like too much, but you'll find out really fast that this is the best way to help your business. And if you were smart and kept following the strategies in this book, you would be outsourcing some areas of your business to free up time and energy to expand your brand's opportunities.

And now, an important warning. Nowadays we are surrounded by noise. We have social media, TV, radio, even videos of cats on the Internet. Everything is designed to distract us. Their business is to get your attention. This means you place time and energy consuming their content rather than focusing on your work.

Yes, you need to have time enjoy, but remember that when you are on business mode, you have to be laser focused. Remember what Donald Trump explained about this matter:

"Don't get sidetracked. If you do get sidetracked, get back on track as soon as possible. Ultimately, sidetracking kills you."

Of course, by "kill you", Mr. Trump means your business. Being always on track while others are distracted will be an important advantage as well.

Finally on this very important topic, Donald Trump's words again:

"I like to think of the word FOCUS as Follow One Course Until Successful."

And:

"When people are in a focused state, the words "I can't," "I'll try," "I'll do it tomorrow," and "maybe" get forced out of their vocabularies."

10

Know the system inside out and take advantage of it.

Do you know how you can bend the rules? The best way is to know them and most important, understand them. This is how you can use them always in your favor and take advantage from them.

In business every little detail is important, most of the big companies fall apart due to not knowing the rules, the small details, the game changers.

Remember: "A tiny leak can sink a ship."

Now… how to do it? Get involved. In this situation you have to be like a coach. Let's place the example of Bill Belichick, someone very respected by Donald Trump as he stated in his Twitter account:

"Never bet against Bob Kraft, Bill Belichick or Tom Brady! @Patriots"

This dynasty trio has become great in good measure because of Brady's talent, but at least 50 percent of their success is due to the perfect knowledge that Bill Belichick has of all the rules in the league. Every week, he has a new perk that the other coaches don't know. Sometimes even the referees are surprised by Belichick's discoveries!

The coach has made this team, which is also a business, into a very profitable brand. Knowing the system and using it to your advantage works exactly the same with your own organization.

How can you manage to get more tax discounts or exemptions? The answer is in the IRS playbook. How to improve the performance of the company? The answer is in your industry itself.

When you understand how things work, you can back-engineer them and then apply the best practices for your own brand. That's how Trump develops business faster than any other entrepreneur in the world.

In his book, **The Art of the Deal**, Trumps says:

"I've always felt that a lot of modern art is a con, and that the most successful painters are often better salesmen and promoters than they are artists."

Why do you think is the reason of this? Exactly. These modern art galleries understood the system and now are making it work in their favor. It's not about art anymore for them, it's about status. Back-engineering of the system and then applying it to their business.

Understanding the system and taking advantage of it is also helpful in planning your goals. As Donald Trump says:

"Remember there's no such thing as an unrealistic goal – just unrealistic time frames"

Having the knowledge of the system you can make very realistic projections for the foreseeable future and be prepared when it comes to obtain as much ROI as possible.

Whenever you know the rules, the system and you use them in your favor, you will be above your competition. They won't be even close to you.

Perhaps the best example of how Mr. Trump has used the system to his benefit has been his campaign to become the President of the United States. Until his arrival, these campaigns had always been the same: secure the funds of some big donors, make friends with the party establishment and some members of the press and say the usual politician thing.

Mr. Trump, however, understood better than anyone that the rules had changed. People were tired of the same faces and the same speeches. In the past, an underdog didn't have a chance to be nominated but 2016 was the year of the underdog.

So he started a campaign, in which the main value was to be independent and to say the things that the other candidates thought but never dared to say, even exaggerating the controversial in order to catch the eye of the people who weren't motivated by politics anymore. The strategy, as we know, was a resounding success. People loved a candidate that finally felt the same way they did, and that offered a glimmer of hope in the shape of "Let's Make America Great Again".

At the moment of publishing this book, the campaign wasn't over but Donald Trump was well on his way to become the Republican Nominee for the 2016 Presidential Election.

11

Be in the right time at the right moment.

In the previous chapter we saw how Donald Trump took advantage of the system to be on his way to be the Republican Candidate for the US Presidency, but that same example applies to his ability to seize the moment. And it would be far from the first time he has done so. So, let's begin this chapter with Donald Trump's words:

"Everything in life is luck."

Donald Trump is always on the move, always pursuing new ventures, he has the right people by his side, he is open to new ideas, he knows the system and makes it work for him but he has never lied about the fact that luck has had a very important role in his career.

Of course, being lucky without being ready is useless. It is like having the chance to get in the coolest pool ever without knowing how to swim. Sooner than later you will drown.

"Luck does not come around often. So when it does, be sure to take full advantage of it, even if it means working very hard. When luck is on your side it is not the time to be modest or timid. It is the time to go for the biggest success you can possibly achieve. That is the true meaning of thinking big."

Donald Trump

Remember The Apprentice? This was a great opportunity for Donald Trump. He made it work because he was open to the idea of making a reality show, but there was no way anyone could have predicted the result. It was a matter of fortune. He placed himself in the right time at the right moment to send his message to a broader audience.

"I could never have imagined that firing 67 people on national television would actually make me more popular, especially with the younger generation."

But he was there and he was prepared to take advantage of it.

Being at the right time at the right moment is a matter of hard work, of being smart. If you follow the strategies in this book you will find yourself or your business in this position very often. And you must always be prepared.

Preparation plus opportunity is how great luck is made. Donald Trump likes to quote Gary Player on this remark:

"The harder you work, the luckier you get."

And of course, he has added some more to the table.

"I am no stranger to working hard. I have done it all my life. As a result I have become accustomed to expecting success in everything I do. Some people call me lucky, but I know better."

Work hard, be prepared and this is inevitable going to lead you to be frequently at the right time at the right moment. Your brand or business will thank you for it.

12

You will fail, so you better learn from it.

"Many people are afraid to fail, so they don't try. They may dream, talk, and even plan, but they don't take that critical step of putting their money and their effort on the line. To succeed in business, you must take risks. Even if you fail, that's how you learn. There has never been, and will never be, an Olympic skater who didn't fall on the ice."

These are words from Donald Trump. He firmly believes them and lives by them. He has proved that as alongside all his successes, he has failed so many times as well. But he has learned from those failures. He has always come back stronger, even after being close to been ruined a couple of times.

"In life you have to rely on the past, and that's called history."

That's how you know how to do things in the moment of doubt. I will let Donald Trump explain it better:

"I try to learn from the past, but I plan for the future by focusing exclusively on the present. That's where the fun is."

When you fail is really not a good feeling, but then, the next time you are faced with a similar challenge you will know exactly how to overcome it and succeed, and that's one of the greatest feelings any businessman can feel.

"In the end, you're measured not by how much you undertake but by what you finally accomplish."

Donald Trump

There has never been an easy path to success. It's human nature to learn from the experience. Sure, we try to minimize the risks with education, but real-life choices and consequences are the ones that teach the most valuable lessons.

"Success comes from failure, not from memorizing the right answers. People who think achieving success is a linear A-to-Z process, a straight shot to the top, simply aren't in touch with reality. There are very few bona-fide overnight success stories. It just doesn't work that way. Success appears to happen overnight because we all see stories in newspapers and on TV about previously unknown people who have suddenly become famous. But consider a sequoia tree that has been growing for several hundred years. Just because a

television crew one day decides to do a story about that tree doesn't mean it didn't exist before."

Donald Trump

So feel reassured that working with the strategies on this book is the right path to success. Your education, added to your experience in the real world of business are going to be your great combo to knock out your competition and elevate the success of your brand and business.

Failure is part of the journey, like Donald Trump explains:

"Think how boring it would be to just sail into things and have everything be perfect. You can't prove your merit on quiet waters, whether you're a businessman or a mariner."

And always remember: taking things one step at the time sometimes is better than trying to handle more than you can, like Donald Trump mentioned in his book The Art of the Deal:

"I could take the greatest deal-makers of all time and they've always had something that didn't quite work out. You never want to put yourself in the position where something not working out is bigger than what you are and therefore takes you down. It's got to be in smaller chunks. In all cases, I want to learn something from things that didn't quite work out and learn, so that it doesn't happen again or so that in the future, you make great decisions. You don't want to make the same mistake twice and you have to learn that early on in your life."

13

Have passion and love for what you do.

"Money was never a big motivation for me, except as a way to keep score. The real excitement is in playing the game."

"I do what I do out of pure enjoyment. Hopefully, nobody does it better. There's a beauty to making a great deal. It's my canvas. And I like painting it."

Donald Trump

Sure, we all want to increase our income to improve our lives. But money can't be your number one reason for doing business. You should be passionate about it. It can be pretty much anything, from painting to sports, or maybe cooking.

Read how Donald Trump feels about Real Estate, which, as you know now, is his main business:

"It's tangible, it's solid, it's beautiful. It's artistic, from my standpoint, and I just love real estate."

Your passion is what will fuel your body and mind to work as much as needed to succeed. Is going to improve you creativity every single team and make your products better.

"I've seen people that are extremely brilliant and they don't have the staying power. They don't have that never give up quality. I've always said that other than bad ideas, which is a reason for failure, the ability to never ever quit or give up is something that is very, very important for success as an entrepreneur."

Donald Trump

Passion is what will put action in your ideas. And ideas plus action equals business, a brand and a whole organization.

When tough times come, if you are not working in something you are really passionate about, any inconvenience will be a good excuse for quitting. After all you don't really care deep down your core.

You have to treat your business or brand as an extension of yourself, and that's by being passionate about it.

Think about the next statement from Donald Trump, and answer, just for yourself, the question he asks in the end:

"Passion is absolutely necessary to achieve any kind of long-lasting success. I know this from experience. If you don't have passion, everything you do will ultimately fizzle out or, at best, be mediocre. Is that how you want to live your life?"

And now, enjoy his own answer to that same question.

"I've known people who had fantastic ideas, but who couldn't get the idea off the ground because they approached everything weakly. They thought that their ideas would somehow take off by themselves, or that just coming up with an idea was enough. Let me tell you something -- it's not enough. It will never be enough. You have to put the idea into action. If you don't have the motivation and the enthusiasm, your great idea will simply sit on top of your desk or inside your head and go nowhere."

14

Between being consistent and being loud, choose being loud.

Donald Trump is a master when it comes to handling the media. It has a lot to do with the way he presents himself. Yes, if you play close attention, you may notice that one day he supports something and maybe the next day he doesn't. It's all part of his strategy.

Sometimes being coherent and plain is good when you are inside your office doing the work required, but is very useless if you want to get more eyeballs looking your way.

Fortunately for you, Trump has already hacked the system and has showed you the way to always get as most exposure as you can possibly have.

The first one is feeding a little bit of controversy. The media loves it because controversy means headlines, which means money for their pockets. So, in the end you can seem like you are doing them a favor.

"One thing I've learned about the press is that they're always hungry for a good story, and the more sensational the better. It's in the nature of the job, and I understand that. The point is that if you are a little different, or a little outrageous, or if you do things that are bold or controversial, the press is going to write about you. I've always done things a little differently, I don't mind controversy, and my deals tend to be somewhat ambitious. Also, I achieved a lot when I was very young, and I chose to live in a certain style. The result is that the press has always wanted to write about me."

Donald Trump

Now, any story is a good story for your business and brand. It's exposure. Even better, it's FREE exposure. And Donald Trump shows you how to handle it.

"I'm not saying that [journalists] necessarily like me. Sometimes they write positively, and sometimes they write negatively. But from a pure business point of view, the benefits of being written about have far outweighed the drawbacks. It's really quite simple. If I take a full-page ad in the New York Times to publicize a project, it might cost $40,000, and in any case, people tend to be skeptical about advertising. But if the New York Times writes even a moderately positive one-column story about one of my deals, it doesn't cost me anything, and it's worth a lot more than $40,000.

The funny thing is that even a critical story, which may be hurtful personally, can be very valuable to your business. Television City is a perfect example. When I bought the land in 1985, many people, even those on the West Side, didn't realize that those one hundred acres existed. Then I announced I was going to build the world's tallest building on the site. Instantly, it became a media event: the New York Times put it on the front page, Dan Rather announced it on the evening news, and George Will wrote a column about it in Newsweek. Every architecture critic had an opinion, and so did a lot of editorial writers. Not all of them liked the idea of the world's tallest building. But the point is that we got a lot of attention, and that alone creates value. . . .

Most reporters, I find, have very little interest in exploring the substance of a detailed proposal for a development. They look instead for the sensational angle."

But you have to make sure you talk straight always when you are dealing with the media. Being evasive and lying never ends well. However, you should guide them to the topics you want to discuss and that are of more benefit for you.

"The other thing I do when I talk with reporters is to be straight. I try not to deceive them or to be defensive, because those are precisely the ways most people get themselves into trouble with the press. Instead, when a reporter asks me a tough question, I try to frame a positive answer, even if that means shifting the ground. For example, if someone asks me what negative effects the world's tallest building might have

on the West Side, I turn the tables and talk about how New Yorkers deserve the world's tallest building, and what a boost it will give the city to have that honor again. When a reporter asks why I build only for the rich, I note that the rich aren't the only ones who benefit from my buildings. I explain that I put thousands of people to work who might otherwise be collecting unemployment, and that I add to the city's tax base every time I build a new project. I also point out that buildings like Trump Tower have helped spark New York's renaissance."

And finally, remember this about your good attributes:

"I call it truthful hyperbole. It's an innocent form of exaggeration — and a very effective form of promotion."

15

Don't waver, keep your goal in mind and go for it!

By this point you have everything you need to become successful. You've read the strategies and tactics to put your business or brand ahead of the competition. But these won't work if you don't start taking action right now.

It's very common to see entrepreneurs doubting about the right time to begin their venture and if you haven't yet noticed after reading all of Trump's experiences in this book, there will never be a right time, so you have to start now. Every minute you let pass by is a new opportunity you won't have back.

So take this advice from Donald Trump, because without this one, the rest won't be useful:

"Get going. Move forward. Aim High. Plan a takeoff. Don't just sit on the runway and hope someone will come along and push the airplane. It simply won't happen. Change your attitude and gain some altitude. Believe me, you'll love it up here."

The time is now. While everyone is being "careful" and try to protect the very little they have you have to be audacious and start your business right now.

Remember. You always have to feel proud about your ventures and make sure you put yourself in the best position to succeed. That means being positive but also having all the necessary precautions for the things that may go wrong.

"Protect the downside and the upside will take care of itself... I happen to be very conservative in business. I always go into a deal anticipating the worst. If you plan for the worst -- if you can live with the worst -- the good will always take care of itself."

So get up your seat. Take your idea to work and hustle your way into the top of your business. This passion of yours will provide you with the greatest satisfaction ever. It will give you stability and it will become your main source of income as well.

If you are not getting the results you want by nowm it has been your fault, even if it's your employees' fault. Remember to always be thinking big, really big, so if your people are not getting you there, you are not surrounded by excellence. For this last part of the book, the next two statements from Donald Trump are the quintessential of The Donald Trump Way and the best way to finish:

"As long as you are going to be thinking anyway, think big.
"Show me someone without an ego, and I'll show you a loser."

"Leaders, true leaders, take responsibility for the success of the team, and understand that they must also take responsibility for the failure."

We began this book talking about taking action and we finished that way. Because what you do is what is going to be what you will get. You are prepared now with the best strategies from the king himself and is now the time for you to create your own kingdom.

Ideas are easy, everyone has ideas, many, every day, the hard part is implementation. You know now the best way to implement and increase your knowledge.

This is the end of the book and the beginning of your journey. I wish you all the success that you are determined to achieve; the same that Mr. Donald Trump has achieved during his crazy and fulfilling life.

Best regards,
Professor Martin Reese.

www.ingramcontent.com/pod-product-compliance
Lightning Source LLC
Chambersburg PA
CBHW061223180526
45170CB00003B/1136